Mother Quiet

Also by Martha Rhodes

Mother Quiet

Martha Rhodes

Zoo Press

Zoo Press • P.O. Box 3528 • Omaha, Nebraska • 68103
Printed in the United States of America

Cover art: The Flower Eater by Robert Henry. By permission
of Sarah Henry

Distributed to the trade by The University of Nebraska Press
Lincoln, Nebraska • 68588 • www.nebraskapress.unl.edu

Library of Congress Cataloging-in-Publication Data

Rhodes, Martha.
  Mother quiet / Martha Rhodes.
     p. cm.
  ISBN 1-932023-18-6 (pbk. : alk. paper)
  1. Mother and child–Poetry. I. Title.

PS3568.H635M68 2004
811'.54–dc22
                                        2004019912

zoo27

First Edition

Acknowledgments

Agni: "The Hose"; *Alaska Quarterly Review*: "Relief" and "Who Sits Behind You"; *American Poetry Review*: "Rheumatic Fever, 1942, my mother recovers," "A Revelation," "Dammit," "Fear Day," "My Body Worn Out from It," "My Brain Was Enormous" and "The Step"; *Barrow Street*: "In the Garbage Can," "Into the Volcano" and "Yes, I Know"; *Columbia*: "Ambassadors to the Dead"; *Expression*: "From the Abandoned"; *Fence*: "A Progression"; *Lit*: "Upon the diagnosis of my nephew,"; *The Marlboro Review*: "If I see her face," "O We," "The Cure" and "The Illness"; *Sad Little Breathings*: "Yesterday, out of the blue,"; *Salamander*: "At the Gate of Phillips Exeter Academy," "Of an Evening" and "20th Year"; *TriQuarterly*: "John," "Migrations," "Our House," "The Restorers" and "This May Be"; *Web Del Sol*: "The After," "Monday at Lunch" and "Mother, Quiet"

"A Progression" was re-printed in *Family*, a catalogue of The Aldrich Museum of Ridgefield, Connecticut. "In the Garbage Can" owes tribute to "The Geranium" by Theodore Roethke.

"Relief" is for Doreen Gildroy.

My gratitude to Sally Ball, Laure-Anne Bosselaar, David Dodd Lee, David Semanki, and Daniel Tobin for their astute comments and support. And special thanks to Joan Aleshire for reading the collection over several years, as it evolved.

In memory, Nan Rhodes

Table of Contents

I

II

I

And we'll get up when we feel
like it, even though mama all luminosity
rouses us with melodious
and charming maternal anger.

—Vallejo, LII *Trilce*

A Progression

I am wearing the last of the sheep.
Winter at the table devouring.
Father torpedoed by hail.
Mother forgetting his name.

I am wearing a necklace of caskets.
April at the table, my birthday.
Father napping, his wallet clutched.
The tip of Mother's nose, white frosting.

I wear a perennial garden.
July at the table perishes. Mother
wants to know who's that Southerner
over there, or is it a lion laughing?

I'm wearing their house around me.
September and the boiler full-blasting.
Father with an axe in the backyard,
Mother in the hallway, maybe.

Yes, I Know

Your mother drools,
your father pees everywhere,
your brother shoots up.
Come on, spare nothing,
tell me how badly
your veins hurt.
You think your heart has moved to the right side.
Enlarged.
Your brain's coated.
You're shedding calcium.
You've misplaced your pulse.
You're pre-emphysemic, agoraphobic, obese,
allergic to sperm.

You hate skin.

Deer tics.
Sciatica.
Murmurs.

You're a tourist in your field of expertise,
spiritually and linguistically impoverished.
You don't dislike your job but you're bad at it.

I know you can't breathe,
fall asleep driving,
recurrently dream of drowning.

Hawaii would be nice.
Venice, better.
Cape Cod a bit too near.
Canada that cold appeal.

Cold as an unlined coffin.
Cold as a dirt-cheap coffin.
Cold as an uncovered coffin.

Yes, you're cold, I know, shhh.

You don't have to tell me more.
I'd prefer it if you'd stop soon,
even better if you'd stop now.
Nice of you, good of you.

Who Sits Behind You?

Who sits behind you? Who, Mother, who do you talk to
louder each day and reach to and sing with in your thin alto voice
and why do you look at me as if I were the unwanted stranger,
as if I would rob you of that napkin you've been shredding since noon—

I want to be the one who holds you, finally, but this stranger
turns you against me—is this the only way you can leave me?

The Step

My mother said my name just now—
with one sock on, her shoes forgotten—
my mother floated down the hall
as I hurried to catch her—
    Mother the step—her cane in my hand—
she went on chattering—she never stops—
    Which one are you?
I held her then but she shoved with her fist—
she wanted something else—not a baby,
not me, middle-aged and grieving, her fist
in my face—something else Mother wanted,
and I just needed her to hold onto one word,
a hopeless wish, that she'd always remember
Martha, her youngest.

Gone

—What the heck! Who stole all the trains?

— I'm taking a bus. Screw this!

— You won't find a bus from here to Milwaukee.

— Call the National Guard someone!

We looked above, into the sky.
No priest in sight. No Hail Marys—

We didn't know what to think. Still don't.

Existence

Catch you later, he called to me
But he didn't, mustn't have tried—
(I was moving so slowly, deliberately)
Level 5
Level 4
To 1
Garage
Sub G
Molten Rock
Though the weight of the world
Is not on my shoulders
Easy to live here

Carefree

My Body Worn Out from It

My body worn out from it   every night.
He comes in   wearing his tux.
He takes it off.   No more No more I cry,
(ecstatically, he thinks).   Not his fault.
He brings me gardens.   Indoors and out.
Long stems. Blossoming trees.   Grasses, bushes,
water gulpers, succulents.   I've not been eating.
Not dressing.   Smell of him 24 hours,
of everything but myself.   I exist only in his head.

When he returns tonight   I'll tell him I can't do much.
Can't taste him.   Won't.

Remorse

While in long sitting
She breathes in their smells.
It's lunch and the young men nap in these bales,
Yet how cold and dry their skin, as if they never received
Her most intimate expressions, just
Last night!

My Brain Was Enormous

My mother died 18 months ago
and I'm tired of checking the calendar.
On what day will I die?
When does my houseguest leave?
When did my calico lose all her teeth
and why did I just notice today?
When will I lose my teeth?

And I'm tired of dust. And coughing—
pneumonia every July.

I miss my mother all day.

We carried her from her room to the hospital bed
in my old room. We surrounded her
with pictures of Aunt Rae, Uncle Billy, her parents,
and us. We spooned ginger ale into her mouth.
We melted ice on her lips and read the hospice pamphlet
for signs of dying. We talked about suffocating her
gently, laying a pillow soft on her face and holding her hands
and talking to her while we did it.

Her breathing was shallow.
The morphine was on fast drip.

Her brain was the size of a shriveled pea.
We were no longer in her brain and hadn't been
for years. For how long, we tried to remember.
When did it begin? There was the morning
she drove across the lawn, through the stone wall,
stopping short of the neighbor's pool; the time
she pulled out onto Thatcher Street too soon;
when she fell on the terrace; when she served
raw crown roast of lamb; when her cheesecake
dripped off our plates; when she cried all night

in my arms; when she visited me in New York
and told me she wanted her life to end; when she first forgot
my name, and my sisters' names; when she fell by the toilet,
when she sang to the toilet for the first time;
when she screamed she was scared to death
and lost, lost, losty posty mosty losty...

The inside of her mouth was black and airless.

The nurse declared her dead, and cleaned her
and sat with her. And put Dad back to bed.

When I visit Dad at the house I sit on the sofa and say, "Hi, Mom."
I want everything of hers I can get. I want to steal
all the pottery, paintings and silver.
My sisters will notice everything gone.
They want to take things too.

Sick last summer, I missed her cool hand
on my forehead and her witch hazel rubdowns.
She was in my brain every second.
My brain was enormous with her.

Such Atmosphere

Can't smell her.
(That's what bothers him most)—
her garden knees, the butter in her laugh —
just inches away she's in their bed! Yet this air
presents her not to him—
rancidness? He'd welcome even that of her.

lavender oil dabbed between your breasts,
behind your ears—

And now their daughter into this room runs,
her mouth and nose covered with (so many)
fingers and scarves—how can this clumsy lady
charge through such atmosphere as this
that carries, propels, transports

not a molecule of you to me.

Ambassadors to the Dead

They're pleased we've come.
Sweets? they offer,
trays of earthened fingers, syrupy.
Join us for a walk. Do.

We've traveled so far already
and what was familiar a moment before —
morphine-glazed now.

We've come to ask about our mother.
We know she'd like to see us. She visited our friend Maria
but not us. We don't understand why. We want to know where
you keep her. We've brought these things for her.
A leaf from her maple tree. Her cranberry cashmere sweater.
We demand to see our mother.
We want this second to talk to our mother.

We accepted no more food, declined their walk,
and the ornaments they offered to hang around our necks —
little skulls they looked like little female skulls.
(They're giving us little heads to wear.)

Plague: Westwood, Massachusetts, Norfolk County

They'll burn our village down.
The bakery, hobby shop, Deer Field Barn.
Fence makers, trench diggers, engineers—dead.

This town is dying, ash and gone.
Black pustules exploding our lungs.
And all the while, not a rat nor flea in sight—

Not found on one body, not the tiniest bite.
The town in blazes, gone—Thatcher Street,
Farm Lane, Route 109, stopped.

Houses and garages upside down,
Emptied onto each front lawn.
The whole lot burnt.

All of us gone.

Into the Volcano

Please,
Stay back.
Breathe. Sweet smoke
My body makes.

II

How ever, the dead are not, cannot be cadavers of a life they have not yet lived. They always died of life.

You're all dead.

–Vallejo, LXXV *Trilce*

Upon the diagnosis of my nephew,

no sun on his soul, just accumulation:

calcium mines, chalk vats, thickening of infidels.
Factories, plazas, warehouses of cells.

And scaling his spine: janitors, lanterns, vacuums,
scrapers, drainpipes, sponges, industrial pails.

Jonathan, Jonny, beloved Jon.
This child sleeps in the gallery of echoes:

Mother, father, sister, and aunts.
Stepmother, grandparents, Wellesley High seniors.

Can he hear us at the window shouting?

O We

Our coffins hurt.
Nurses bring babies.

Little girls—briefly.
Much milk and tears.

Each soul alone
In the naked field.

God unable to enter.
Is he among the lilies

Delivered to our doors?

The Illness

flies over us and all we
possess—nothing heals—

our doctors the first to flee.

It is the oceans and mountains that crawl
to us now—the sun and moon which fall

at our feet and God in the fields, digging.

Mother, Quiet

I, too, felt chased, hunted —
so when I passed your room
I didn't stop for you,
didn't lift and carry you
out of that "pit"
I heard you call it,
that square, that bed.

Up into my arms I did not bring you,
there, there, I did not say, Mother,
quiet, I've got you now.

If I see her face,

her hands lying there, the gash of gangrene huge
across her stomach, blue and upturned on the river—

if I see what has been described to me this short week,
all week, all night, all day—the brokenness, the way

she kissed the air goodbye as rescuers stood beside—
a hundred times since Tuesday I've walked to town center

looking for her to tell me she is still here, with us—

if I see her I will hum her quickly toward me, and soon
the bridge will sway and buckle, the weight of us all

and all of us singing, too much to endure—the Charles below
thick from the barricade of our bodies, this gentle river

backed up solid from Millis to Dedham, swollen now,
its miles of willows tumbling.

Rheumatic Fever, 1942, my mother recovers

at a farm in New Hampshire—her parents
playing bridge in Miami—sent here to rest
with sheep-for-slaughter and a farmer whose wife
dies under him two times a night—my mother
can hear it all—some haven, this
inland sea of frozen fields, gnarled
grasslands, Mother in the attic
tinted by a weak sun, small
radiation each afternoon—
                    and then, to Florida,
delivered—wartime, blinds down, curfew,
hidden jazz clubs, and my father, slick,
met for the first time—forbidden liquor,
weed, and savage dreams—torn glory
in the piano bar's upper rooms and everywhere
it's hurricane season (ruins of terror,
ruins of delight), dark wreckage of his car—
they walk toward the waves, beggars at the shore
for more rain, more wind, more pounding, more love.

Of an Evening

Nothing to do.
The black bog croaking in the distance,
the town carnival dying down for the night,
damp air from the road below entwining them—

Sleep with her?
Here? On the Immaculate
porch of her father's house?

Better be Careful—Christ he'll be Careful—

carry her tender through the gaudy gate
to the end of the lane's soft grass, at this hour
everything calling.

The After

Fifteen years, no calls, no letters
and now he comes home, walks right in,

his father just one-hour dead, seizure
then silent. All night this son

perfectly calm, a warm flood
within him—"Quite dead,"

his family heard him whisper—
"Quite dead!" next morning as he leapt

from the porch laughing his way
toward their northern tree-line—

"Gone," his mother often sighs,
decanting wine, carving up turkey—

"Quite gone," his sisters and their husbands
nod and chew, and his nephews and cousins—

even the ones far removed.

Our House

Ours is the only all glass house in the state.
Tourists from everywhere come to see, especially
a guy from Worcester.

He yells from his car, *Hey honey, walk down the hall*
to the bathroom again and do that little thing you do
when you adjust your skirt—

Ours is the only all glass house in the world, my oldest sister moans.

My teacher says our house is a bow wow house! I announce one night.

That's Bauhaus, dear, our mother says, *and goodness, it's not.*

My friends love our house. My friends love ME! my middle sister boasts.

Remember, girls, it's the interior of the house that's of import,
Father proclaims. *To find one's riches, one must look within.*

Indeed we do, dear, Mother says, *we do do that.*

Fear Day

His almost mother
And his (this) father
Ensnarled think,

Fear. Fear on this fabulous day!
Fear is what they want this day to be about.
Yes, Fear's on their written plan

For this day out, circling
Their picnic, grabbing the son
(And son's friend) by the afternoon

And dumping them headfirst into the red Mazda trunk.
Just for a minute dearies, (the almost mother says),
We'll let you out soon.

Glorious day for Fear, the two adults neck,
Thinking about having another kid or two or three —
Little barbed bald kids —

To take on Sundays to the park!
After all, your son isn't mine, she says.
And her breasts extend toward him

Like two he doesn't know whats
But they're friendly and bobbing in his face
And he's going to do something with them.

He just doesn't know how/when.

The Promise

You promised I'd get better
when he died and you promised
he would die—that I'd be
less attracted to knives,
the delicate underside
where my wrist and forearm speak,
the downward slope of belly—

When I was young he'd die each day,
and all the Pleasant Valley dads
presented themselves to me! Lining up
on our terrace for mimosa-scented
breakfasts, lunches, entire
Saturdays—but now he doesn't even
shut his eyes—he won't go to bed,
just sits in that chair (by midnight it's wet)

and refuses to depart, yet
he wants to, doesn't he?
Depart? So miserable
his gloomy wonderings:
who stirs cyanide into his tea,
which daughter chants voodoo to his likeness—
this second his feet and ears sting, look,
red spots up his arms—
        is it me doing that? Me? His body
        this cushion of needles in my palm?

You promised me and you swore
he would not be God's sole exception.

The Hose

A hose ran through our house, used
to wash our windows down; to keep
us teenagers in line; to dilute Father's
martoonis; "to make life a little more
exciting," Mother said.

When Mother turned 70 and renamed us
"Enormous One," and
"One Who Walks Bare on Rug,"
and "One Who Hideously Shares My Bed,"
and "Which One"

we hosed her into the corner of her dressing room—
Strong Medicine.
Clean out the cobwebs.
Cold showers are a cure-all.
Shock therapy.

Mother would giggle herself silly when we'd towel her dry,
dust her with powder, pull the bedrails up.

Yesterday, out of the blue,

in the room of much crying
he held them up to me —
babies.

He gave me some babies to keep!

Today, when I told him,
"Y'know, I'm actually good with children,
really good,
and I'm moving with these kids
to Sag Harbor   or Wellfleet,"
he told me I'm "such a child"
and took the babies back.

A Revelation

Don't waste your time talking normally to people who aren't normal, TH offered, so I stopped.

To my sister: *Maybe you could visit Mom more often, do some... shopping...*

Became: *Blabbeddy-blah, blabbeddy-blah, non-pop-ka'poop.* Much easier, TH right again.

Mom remains infrequently visited but I am happier in most relationships, especially with my sister. Last Thanksgiving, a breeze.

The Gift of April

What can I tell you of my birthstone—
ignorant daughter of the jeweler
who sweetened my cereals
with the sparkles of April.

I who cut my teeth on them
swallowed many. Little chips
punched into my ears,
boulders I have lost mountains. ← *punctuation?*

When

When our children smelled of perfume,
our perfume smelled of skin.
Our skin smelled of hedges
and our hedges smelled of wings.
Then our wings smelled of injuries.
Our injuries smelled of river, a river
smell of yellow and our children
ran away.

In the Garbage Can

Terrible, alone,
in the window, wilted, filled up
once a week only, and only if she remembers—
then thrown out, frozen, smothered in the garbage can,
leafless, waiting for the truck to shuttle you to that
Mountain in Queens—

What does it feel like this second?
(Fantastic, right?) to be free of her neglect?

← NICE ELLIPSIS FOR METAPHOR

SPEAKER?

From the Abandoned

The house we're walking by? Someone else's.
And every car parked on this street, too.
And that street.
This black lab and her calico neighbor. That Springer Spaniel.
That, that, that. Even that bench.
Boots! Black, brown, pairs mud-caked on newspaper, not ours.
Baseball bat. Basketball hoops above every single driveway.
Barbie, headless, sticking out from the abandoned
Birdcage in the window—someone else's, else's.
Blossoms, too. Ivory, pink-edged magnolia blossoms, too.

Monday at Lunch

This booth is reserved for me.
This booth is endowed by me.
Not enough that you serve me
promptly today, smilingly—
I'm less hungry today than Monday
at lunch, when I needed you.
I was shaking and you didn't see
how many sugar packets I'd emptied
into my palms. I licked my palms
as if there was no tomorrow.
I wasn't sure there would be a tomorrow.

You! Behind the house!

Drop my sofa
My stove
My nephew
My clippers
My cats My husband
My frenzy

The Cure

All of us ill—especially
The men—

Mad rage, bloodshed
Against the red, earthen wall—

Hadn't we heard it? The contagion
Coming down our chimneys?

Hadn't we escaped? Yes,
Our lonely wagons, yes,

Prairie in every direction—by noon
We'll reach the creek—

That wonderful, endless, shimmering milk.

The Restorers

We saw them in the hedges
gathering our injuries,
their tender wings
lifted what they could.
Field flowers perfum'd our acres
and we no longer smelled of death.
Our skin lost that yellow cast.
We would be a town again—
houses, lawns,
children at the fairgrounds.

Relief

The churchyard, flooded.
Your prompt arrival—

White carriage, your wheels bright
as you flatten this pine-needled route.

And how pleasant the way
you've found my house (I couldn't have)

and pass through the gate as if it isn't
even there, perhaps it isn't,

but the baby I hear singing is surely
here, yes? she, the one you really came for—

I am happy you remembered I'd be waiting too.

This May Be

This may be the room you lived in,
but do not fill it, tiny ghost. Do not fill
the blooming shadow we call "our garden."
Grey Faced One, go somewhere else
and do not fill these winter flowers, do not fill
this drying sea sponge, do not stand beside
our bed tonight, do not fill our ears with glitter.

III

It hails so much, as if to make me recall
and increase the pearls
that I've gathered from the very snout
of every storm.

–Vallejo, LXXVII, *Trilce*

Closing the House

Gone you've been from its plaster and cork,
from this bench I take, this painting of the boat.

Your wooden spoons, cutting boards,
coming with me, just as you wished.

Calm down, please dear, Mother, Mother,
it's been three years... yes, that's right,

you've found your way back, you can stay or leave,
but Mother, please hush, I need to *work*.

Hope

I pluck marshweed from this pasture of rhinestones,
The paperbirds (I've shaped!) ring through the orchards—

I have been so lonely in my kitchen trembling, Good Lord
I'll do almost anything now, in the spring, my substance bloated.

Nectarines

That summer she suspected
she'd be alone. She would order him away
and she suspected

each day his bare feet up
on somebody's velvet sofa,
nectarines dripping

all over him—she suspected
his feet,
suspected velvet, nectarines,

and everything that dripped
from anything—she expected
no one to kiss her that summer

and that summer would lead
to all seasons—she'd been a fool
and realized might remain one,

not telling him finally to leave,
keeping him at home, with her,
on the sofa she suspected.

Dammit!

She was

In the

Which then

Had died

Her nose

Told her

"Between us

It's Dead"

Was she

Crazy? Felt.

But him

She wanted

Any way,

All positions,

In out,

Hard deep,

Sex was

All they

Could then.

Now what?

Now what?

Honey Honey,

It's me.

All yours.

What's wrong?

You mad?

We've always

Fixed things

Our past

Got better

So why now, huh?

Migrations

1.

Through the paper hall
both of them fly,

or lie down.

In the paper hall's where they'll lie —
both of them fly

to where they'll lie (opposite corners).

Why
lie to me? she cries.

I'm telling the truth, he lies
through his paper teeth, on fire now.

2.

Hard not to trip handing
him his coffee—

her face in his wet, hot lap.

3.

Ordered by her to leave forever
he eyes the wallpaper *he* chose and pasted.

She bought the curtains to match the paper.
Oh, can't they just continue like this—

her drapes, his walls.

4.

My wife kept bees, he'll tell his girlfriend (when he has one).

When she liked me, was pleased with me, the bees just buzzed.
But when she didn't… oh boy. One time she ordered them
to circle a bowl of lemons and sting so many times juice overflowed.
Was terrifying. I couldn't stand it.
So many cruelties. I had to leave…

To which the girlfriend will undoubtedly reply, *Of course you left,*
my poor stung boy. Who could stand it? So many cruelties
you endured.

5.

and quiet, light as a hush
he tells me   what?

Speak up.
Oh speak up.

And again, even quieter, lighter
than hush, he tells me   what? What
is he saying?   What?

And lighter, softer than hush
he tells me if he wanted me to hear him

I'd hear him.

6.

A few days
Of *Moaning*
And I'm now
Better
Up from this bed

How I needed to be still
And suffering!

At the Gate of Phillips Exeter Academy

is where I ended up,
nude, maybe, and ripe,
pungent, waiting for him and his hash pipe
to show—oh where the hell was he?
Lewis!
Not even on time for my dreams.

John

He (please don't tell) is the one man in my life
(almost 70 now?) I've ever wanted to grab by the belt buckle
and ride so fast the bed would take off.
But I'd just sit there, all those interminable nights
at the Center for the Arts, my thigh grazing his—
through high school, Lucy and I drove to Cambridge
in my mother's car, hid a few houses from his,
and followed him to the clinic where he worked,
then to all his Saturday chores.
We'd haunt Café Algiers.
When Lucy died he called me.
When I met my husband, I called him.
I can tell he has come to New York.
I can feel him walking in New York,
I can feel him walking up my block
and stopping to buy water
and looking up my building
up the 40 floors up through my floor
up between my legs
up through my head

20th Year

He took the porch.
She built a deck.
In the middle of the night
he took the deck.
He planted a vineyard of bitters.
She mowed a clearing.
She installed a cage around it
with a "Beware!" sign.
He arrived with six pals
who all morning sawed at the cage.

She drove to his new bungalow
ready to throw buckets of blood
but when she saw her front porch
and back deck, her lawn chairs,
a glass of lemonade on the top step
looking full and cool, she sat and drank,
their children (or another couple's) somehow
around her in swing chairs, at play, and her husband,
though it rained, at the distant corner of the yard,
cutting peonies for their nightstands,
for both sides of their bed.

The Retrieval

Leave that in the bedroom. It'll keep.
Dessert.

What we need now is out there,
in our yard—

the green bottle we buried,
the message inside.